WALTON WELL

CULTURE ART POETRY FICTION SOCIAL JUSTICE

PRESS

THE H.D. SEQUENCE—
A CONCORDANCE

ALSO BY SARAH MACLAY

COLLECTIONS

Nightfall Marginalia

The "She" Series: A Venice Correspondence
(with Holaday Mason)

Music for the Black Room

The White Bride

Whore

LIMITED EDITION CHAPBOOKS

Ice from the Belly

Shadow of Light

Weeding the Duchess

A SCRIPT TO PERFORM

Fugue States Coming Down the Hall

THE H.D. SEQUENCE— A CONCORDANCE

Sarah Maclay

WALTON WELL PRESS
Los Angeles   Oxford

Cover Art: Hieronymus Bosch, *The Garden of Earthly Delights* (1503–1515),
oil on oak panels, (81 in x 152 in), Museo del Prado, Madrid.

Cover Design & Typesetting: ash good

Published by Walton Well Press
Los Angeles | Oxford
Editor: Theresia de Vroom

Paperback ISBN: 978-1-964295-05-3

WALTONWELLPRESS.COM

A Brief Introduction

These pieces in *The H.D. Sequence—A Concordance* often felt, as they were emerging, more like glimpses, fragments, bouncing off of phrases in the center of Hilda Doolittle's *Trilogy*, which I was teaching at the time I began writing this, and which became a bit of a lifeboat and north star, particularly her section 29 in *Tribute to the Angels*, with its many recastings of the figure of Mary. For those of you who might be new to H.D.—so christened by her close compadre and first love Ezra Pound ("H.D. Imagiste"), she became one of the key Modernist poets, an American writing largely from Europe and, in the poems of *Trilogy*, largely while living in the ravaged and unpredictable London of the second World War, and she was associated mainly with the Imagist movement. In works like *Trilogy*, she moves from those more strictly Imagist impulses, which can be almost haiku-like in their precision and distillation, into long, linked sequences that are highly allusive, informed by Biblical and painterly imagery and figures and a keen interest in earlier cultures and myths, as well as the practical and spiritual concerns and conundrums pressing on her in her distressing present.

Orignally, these came as hot bursts, urgent for survival but still very fragmented. And out of such a hot original impulse, such immediate need . . . I'm not sure if what remains is something we could call "disobedient" or simply unruly, half-formed, unwilling, apparently, to form itself differently. Begun sort of ferociously in a many-poems-all-at-once frenzy, during a season of sudden emotional duress, this manuscript was also often in continuous contact with H.D.'s work, as many of her phrases became my routes toward incipient healing, and so found their way into the work as poem titles or sometimes borrowed language within a poem. In this way, it was like being in some kind of conversation with her *Trilogy*, especially "29," and though I know this bends the word a little, I can't think of "Concordance" now without special emphasis on the last syllable. In a way, it was like I was dancing with her words, which were also very centering—a kind of dancing while being stilled. These pieces are also fed by dream and artwork, as so often happens with me. This took a long time to complete because, after that initial rush of poems, I was so rarely in such raw turmoil that it wasn't really possible to jimmy a place like that to work from—an emotional state— or, on the other hand, I would get these *notions*—about trying this or that—that wouldn't really work, because they were coming from too conceptual a place, but I finally realized that I was farther along than I'd thought, and somehow I was finally able to *see* it again clearly enough to be able to finish the waiting germs of poems (or *parts* of this whole, which may be more accurate) and to trust the few much newer things that felt right for this sequence.

    —S. Maclay

Parts

and the sea-foam
marks the sea-path
where no sea ever comes . . .

—H.D., "Projector"

Our Lady of the Goldfinch

Just one—yellow, yes, seemingly lonely

on her lap. Though she pets it, though the color

    is complicated by others—darker ones,

even against the morning's orange air . . .

      and then the striped wings in a child's hand.

                  Two slender, distant trees.

    And there are boys. The whole truth lying

on the grass. The rock they sit on—browning

      like a velvet moss, bugs and petals crowding bare

feet. A net of pine.

    She can imagine someone,

           someone to tell.

And sky, somehow, ripping through the fabric of a cloud,

    her dress. As though her clothing tears from the inside, begins

to shred.

      Everything needs stitching.

            And night shows through—

      in glimpses

if we could see its cracks (and needles

    needles

                      needles

      needles

        across the entire canvas).

Our Lady of the Candelabra

But I imagine her wearing it on her head like a hat—like Goya—

      like a Norwegian lutefisk celebration, middle of winter.

Every time the head moves, a danger of fire.

Also a danger of light.

Prologue (as I currently understand it)

It was the anger door
  and she opened it.

      Remember the Renaissance beauty
          and her quilted face?

  That blindfold of Tiffany barbed wire,
      a bracelet for the eyes?

      Well, in another painting the blindfold was silk, red silk—

  her double (her sister?) in profile,
walking behind her.

Question: was the Mona Lisa also
  zipped into a metal shroud?

  She had been a painting once.

There was a he, too,
  when she could (remember to)
      make him out.

He suffered.

In his body—were those knives
  or bowling pins?

    And had she thrown the knives?

Sometimes he was distance.

      Tobacco rolled like a boat
          or a pair of insect wings
at his back.

Or was she the dancer?

       (The dancer, the target—
the dress of Belgian lace,

arachnid-like,
         behind her—

         look closely at the eyes:
moths have gotten to the netting.)

Like a cast-off shell,
    she ghosted forward.

Our Lady of the Pomegranate

Not just one. She's studded with them. So's her throne.

    Her throne, all silk and red. Split open. And some would say apples
but maybe it's really this fruit that she's bound to with string—

        five strings. One for each finger. Five fruits. And something that bleeds
not just onto the page, as she slits the plump seeds, and stares at the art

           deco sketch of a nymph eating seeds, but that bleeds
more and more—more than it should, from within, staining

      the several grades and softnesses and thicknesses of paper,
wadded inside and out, and cloth that she wears on her body

        and sheets (though she tries to relinquish, to wash out

    the stain).

trapped in a golden halo

It was simply too snug.

    Plus it had always looked as though it were made of actual gold,

like a platter,

        so it must be heavy

though she carried herself with grace,

                erect, as if from practicing, as a child,

walking across the living room with a book on her head.

or the apple-russet silk

This is the leisure of wanted silk / the wanted leisure of silk.

    We can nearly taste it. We can hear it rustle

as she moves, as she must,

        eventually. And below the silk, there must be crinoline

petticoats. And below the petticoats, apples, shining, dangling, growing

    in size as she walks, winesaps, golden delicious, fuji, mac,

as though strapped to her body,

        green, transparent, gala, their stems abrading her legs—

apples full of juice and hard brown seeds and the choking waxiness of cores

    and bottoms, dark as navels.

And, in another room, the sound of a bite.

. . . *in fine silks—*

doves in a very large cage, cooing, beyond the sofas

stripped of upholstery

to get to the padding below.

at the turn of the palace stair

It was a place that had the feeling of marble, of time. Hors d'oeuvres

all around, some harps. Proffering the chance of

a later meal, he'd gathered a group of women together:

if anyone had happened to bring a set of packed bags, well, she

(and he) could go to Paris, instead.

                                        One of them had.

with arrow

This is where the confusion comes in, between Cupid
and deer.

. . . the suave turn of the head

is what she'd imagined, hoped for. Then the photographer

snapped her picture:

>the one now titled

"Holding Her Name Upside Down On A Sign."

They were all wearing black; cameras and umbrellas

>parked on a landing by the men's room,

everything white and gray——the worn industrial rug, the walls.

>Nonetheless, the photos were in color, though the only shot

she liked was the one where she was glancing down so far

>that her eyes looked actually closed——just as though she were really

almost sleeping.

head bowed / with the weight
of a domed crown

how she wept into the pillow cushions of the couch,

    apologizing, post-thanksgiving, helpless with merlot

and her head sank further into the cushions.

    The next day, she'd dump the rest of the turkey,

in its silver sack.

her snood / drawn over her hair

or the furry North Dakota hat with forehead flaps and ears—

the right thing, in this moment, to wear to a party—

     and not remove. The need to be anti-fetching.

The need to shake the Crystal

     Geyser water and spray

like a dog, jumping into a hydrant,

     summer all over her clothing, the plates, her hands,

until someone could help her remove the cap

     or the pressure stopped, the pressure

stopped.

actually, at the turn of the stair

But this is the one she needed—this visitation, this vision, a sense of light,

    a presence, a wing—not a real wing—

a kind of light, sound of sun burned through the moon

    (gentler than anything she could now imagine):

something beyond violence

    and something beyond violence to self—

        beyond the feeling, even, of being in her own legs,

though that was streamingly intense now.

    She wanted something beyond all spectrums

she had ever known. What,

    anyway, is light?

her hand at her throat

It was unconscious, nearly: simply the way, in the midst of a thought,

she'd stroke her throat for a second—

as though it were the guy wire keeping all the electricity

from belting/bursting/escaping into the sky.

Really, it was not a dire gesture—

not that.

Like something a dog would do in the middle of sleep.

Except more graceful.

It countered the also-unconscious furrow above her brow that was more like a

river bed, actually, than anything in a field.

with doves / and a heart like a valentine

but why did we see this, too, in a cage?

Her rage, as bright as a trumpet,
    filled her stomach with a sound
that took the place of food
      but she was glad, at least,
it filled her stomach—
  and not the air in front of her—
     though it would have emerged
as loud as a claxon, a siren—
             bigger than miles.
And the owners—
   because there are always owners—
would have to decide what to do
     with their non-performing cage.

we see her stare past a mirror /
through an open window

It's a moment in which she's solid enough not to bother

with verification. The mirror, suddenly, holds little interest—

      just a piece of glass or metal on a wall.

As though it were tradition, here, to hang such things as trinkets.

Windows: other trinkets. Walls.

Our Lady of Wrong Lyrics

He demands, the landlord, pugnacious, with strangely cut hair

    (as though cut in clumps and darkened), that she write the lyrics

for his musical (in which some biblical backstory/message

       is braided with urban violence) or be killed. By him. To demonstrate,

he kills his wife, who has also refused, in the next room,

         allowing her to listen. She imagines chunks of melons

thunking, rolling pins, or bats. The project holds no interest.

   She asks about credit, which she would normally receive,

and he says that the lyrics must be ghost-written, that the music

    will come second. To her surprise, this comes as a great relief

(the project holds no interest), in particular because it gives her

    freedom to write badly, to destroy his project, to write in a mediocre

voice, anonymously, with the conviction that he cannot tell

      the difference. Nonetheless, she begins to conceive of ways in which

to leave the apartment, piece by piece, at lunchtimes, say, or times

    when he's not there, carrying her belongings one by one,

  until the room she lives in is bare

      and she can simply disappear, for good.

Our Lady of the Chair

It will not be electric,

not for this exercise.

It's a simple chair,

a calm chair.

Wooden.

in a wooden room.

Nothing else

in the room.

Nothing in the chair

that we can see.

Our Lady of Cicadas

or locusts.

I had thought for many years

that they were birds.

That she gathered sticks

for firewood, carried like long poles

across the center of her body.

That she dressed in black

habitually. Passing other stacks

of sticks or palm debris, the sheaves

of something less than wood

but more than leaf. That she carried

these long sticks through silent streets, white

stucco walls. But it was a cemetery.

And the monuments, as large as houses.

And the dress, for mourning.

And not streets were vacant,

but the rows. And not birds,

not birds . . .

Our Lady of the Snow

Horizontal:

flying needles lashing against the windshield, night,

                                                        sewing

east to west.

          To be *not* ash—

every fleck a piece of fire

made pure by its own burning.

That is, to fall like manna—

far beyond one thing

we can identify as body.

To be the entire snowfall—

          for the entire time.

This was the desire,

          if not the vision.

and in her lap / smoothing the apple-green—

the color of her new sweater,

which went with the green of her eyes,

intensified them—though, often as not,

she was smoothing the cat—

with a single flower / or a cluster of
garden-pinks / in a glass beside her

with the blue hood and stars—

and the way that midnight is a kind of hat for hiding in.

Afterlogue

                   (because we must make our own poultice

        even beyond the solace of beauty):

What she got instead:

a luncheon visit from the neurosurgeon

    and his wife—

she knew then that he studied his own brain

          because he left the folds exposed

for all to see below a mop of hair

             (the wall sculptures

        kept wafting just like soft balloons

                  or hands):

she got to watch them long enough

to see them.

Notes

The italicized phrases that appear as titles, and many of the additional italicized phrases within these poems, are drawn from H.D.'s 29th and 30th poems in "Tribute to the Angels," the second part of her *Trilogy*.

I've received additional inspiration for some of these poems from spending time looking at paintings by Pam Hawkes and Raphael, and photographs of Eric Michelson and Graciela Iturbide, in particular, her "Cemeterio," the key inspiration for "My Lady of Cicadas."

Acknowledgments

Versions of these pieces first appeared in the following publications:

Al-Khemia Poetica: "Our Lady of the Goldfinch" and "Our Lady of the Chair"

Into Discourse: "in fine silks . . . ," "with arrow," "actually, at the turn of the stair," and "and in her lap / smoothing the apple-green,"

The Laurel Review: "Our Lady of the Snow" and "Afterlogue"

Nashville Review: "Our Lady of the Pomegranate," "Our Lady of the Candelabra" and "or the apple-russet silk"

Poemeleon: "her snood / drawn over her hair," "head bowed / with the weight of a domed crown" and "trapped in a golden halo"

Slope: "with doves / and a heart like a valentine," "her hand at her throat . . ." and "we see her stare past a mirror / through an open window"

Zocalo Public Square: "Our Lady of Wrong Lyrics" and "Our Lady of Cicadas"

Parts of the introduction also appear in *Poemeleon: The Disobedient Issue* and in an interview for *The Tampa Review.*

About the Author

Sarah Maclay is the author of five collections of poetry—most recently, *Nightfall Marginalia* (What Books Press), a 2023 Foreword INDIES Finalist—and three previous chapbooks. Published widely, her work has been supported and honored by a Yaddo residency, a City of Los Angeles Individual Artist Fellowship, the *Tampa Review* Prize for Poetry and a Pushcart Special Mention, appearing in *APR, FIELD, Ploughshares, The Writer's Chronicle, The Best American Poetry* series, *Poetry International*, where she served as Book Review Editor for a decade, and elsewhere. She has taught creative writing and literature at LMU and USC, and offers periodic workshops at Beyond Baroque. Website: www.sarahmaclay.com

* 9 7 8 1 9 6 4 2 9 5 0 5 3 *